God's Grace from Place to Place

Moving with the Spirit

Student

Robin Harris Kimbrough
Abingdon Press/Nashville

God's Grace from Place to Place: Moving with the Spirit

Student Book

Production Team: Marilyn E. Thornton, Matthew Orozco, Alean Biles

Copyright 2009 by Abingdon Press

All Rights Reserved

No part of this work may be reproduced or transmitted in any form or by any means, electronic or mechanical, including photocopying and recording or by any information storage or retrieval system, except as may be expressly permitted by the 1976 Copyright Act or in writing from the publisher. Requests for permission should be addressed to Abingdon Press, P.O. Box 801, 201 Eighth Avenue, South, Nashville, TN 37202-0801.

All Scripture quotation unless otherwise noted are taken from the New Revised Standard Version of the Bible, copyright 1989, Division of Christian Education of the National Council of Churches of Christ in the United States of America. Used by permission. All rights reserved.

Scripture quotations noted NIV are taken from the Holy Bible, New International Version. Copyright 1973, 1978, 1984 by the International Bible Society. Used by permission of Zondervan Publishing House. All rights reserved.

This book is printed on acid-free, elemental-chlorine-free paper.

Library of Congress Cataloging-in-Publication Data
ISBN 978-0-687-65518-2

09 10 11 12 13 14 15 16 17 18--- 10 9 8 7 6 5 4 3 2 1

CONTENTS

Introduction 4-5

Lesson One *An Unlikely Leader:*
Moving with God Towards Justice 7-13

Lesson Two *The Suffering Servant:*
Moving with God Towards Greatness 14-20

Lesson Three *God's Abundant Kingdom:*
Moving with Jesus Towards Blessing 21-26

Lesson Four *True Treasure:*
Moving with God Towards Truth 27-32

Lesson Five *Grace, Love, and Justice:*
Moving with Jesus Towards Reconciliation 33-40

INTRODUCTION

This adult Bible study, *God's Grace from Place to Place: Moving with the Spirit*, focuses on how God's Spirit gave momentum to the Civil Rights Movement in different places, drawing the people of God towards greatness in soul through blessing, justice, truth, and reconciliation. Even as the study stands on its own merits, these lessons can also serve as a follow up to *Walk Together Children: Taking a Stand for God*. They continue to weave together biblical story, modern history, contemporary events, and 21st century concerns so that the people of God can be equipped for Kingdom living and building, in making disciples for Jesus Christ in order to transform God's world.

Even as it tells and interprets Bible story and teaching for 21st century postmoderns *God's Grace from Place to Place: Moving with the Spirit* utilizes **On the Road to Freedom: A Guided Tour of the Civil Rights Trail** by Charles E. Cobb, Jr. (2008)* as a heritage source. Charlie Cobb was on his way to college when he got "kidnapped by the Movement." He became a community organizer in Mississippi with SNCC and was an eyewitness to how people of faith sacrificed to make life better and create change for future generations. In his book, he focused on lesser-known events/places and personalities, especially women, demonstrating the widespread activity of the Movement. There was Gloria Richardson who sat down with the brothers Kennedy to negotiate an agreement for the people of Maryland Eastern Shore. And there was Septima Poinsette Clark who taught thousands in literacy schools in order to prepare them for voter registration. And then, there was Irene Morgan who was actually the first, in 1943, to refuse to give up her bus seat. Additionally, there was Hosea Williams who stood on a rock like Moses stood and Myles Horton, who provided a place for organizers to be trained in safety in the hill country of Tennessee.

From Joseph, the slave, to the woman, Deborah, to Jesus, son of a carpenter, the Bible is full of unlikely leaders for God who moved with God towards justice, greatness, blessing, truth and reconciliation. Joseph's development demonstrates how God can use any situation to mold persons towards greatness in God. The story of how Paul and John Mark's broken relationship moved towards reconciliation is a reminder of how the Holy Spirit moves to heal our brokenness so that we may experience community in Jesus Christ. With these lessons, participants will discover the movement of God's grace through events in time and move towards a desire for the movement of the Holy Spirit in their lives as they aspire to greatness of soul in Jesus Christ!

The word "towards," which is often interchangeable with "toward" (no "s") is used throughout this study because it has the additional meaning as follows: "indicates imminent or expected attainment of a goal."** With God we move in the expectation of reaching the destination. With God, it is already done. Joseph, the slave was destined for greatness. What others meant for evil, God meant for good. He moved with God towards greatness!

Through video, song, and discussion (as designated by the icon ⌣) the lessons are designed to keep interest during Bible Study time. Additionally, there are projects and seminar questions (see leader book) for the continuing engagement of individuals and community for future weeks and months, understanding that as people of faith, we are moving with God, by the power of the Holy Spirit towards a beloved community in Jesus Christ. We pray "Thy kingdom come" as we live into the realization of the Kingdom by studying and spreading the good news of God's deliverance and reconciliation to and for all people.

> Marilyn E. Thornton
> Lead Editor of African American Resources
> Contributing Editor for *God's Grace from Place to Place*

---

* Unless otherwise noted, all quotes in the lessons are from ***On the Road to Freedom: A Guided Tour of the Civil Rights Trail*** by Charles E. Cobb, Jr. (NY: Algonquin Books, 2008).

** ***The American Heritage Dictionary of the English Language***

Note: Prayers are by the Rev. Dr. Safiyah Fosua, Director of Invitational Preaching Ministries of the General Board of Discipleship (UMC).

Session #1

An Unlikely Leader: Moving with God Towards Justice

Judges 4:4-10

Key Verse *And the Israelites came up to her for judgment.(Judges 4:5b)*

Opening Prayer
Sovereign God, help us to keep an open ear to your summons to service. Lord, call our names; move us towards justice; send us. Help us to know that we are the ones that we have been looking for. In the name of Jesus Christ. Amen.

BIBLE LESSON

At that time Deborah, a prophetess, wife of Lappidoth, was judging Israel. She used to sit under the palm of Deborah between Ramah and Bethel in the hill country of Ephraim; and the Israelites came up to her for judgment. She sent and summoned Barak son of Abinoam from Kedesh in Naphtali, and said to him, "The LORD, the God of Israel, commands you, 'Go, take position at Mount Tabor, bringing ten thousand from the tribe of Naphtali and the tribe of Zebulun. I will draw out Sisera, the general of Jabin's army, to meet you by the Wadi Kishon with his chariots and his troops; and I will give him into your hand.' Barak said to her, "If you will go with me, I will go; but if you will not go with me, I will not go." And she said, "I will surely go with you; nevertheless, the road on which you are going will not lead to your glory, for the LORD will sell Sisera into the hand of a woman." Then Deborah got up and went with Barak to Kedesh. Barak summoned Zebulun and Naphtali to Kedesh; and ten thousand warriors went up behind him; and Deborah went up with him.

CALLED TO LEAD (Judges 4:4)

In the fourth chapter of Judges, we meet Deborah, one of the most heroic persons in the history of Israel. This wife and prophetess was an unlikely hero because she was a woman. On one hand, Scripture does not point out Deborah's leadership as being unusual. The situation is described in a simple, a-matter-of-fact manner: "At that time Deborah, a prophetess, wife of Lappidoth, was judging Israel." On the other hand in Scripture, women had to sue for their inheritance (Numbers 27:1-11), birthing girls required twice the purification time as birthing boys (Leviticus 12), and men routinely gave up the women in their homes to be raped (Genesis 12:10-20, Genesis 19:1-8, Judges 19) and maimed. Women were mostly devalued and viewed as property and not normally placed in leadership roles.

Unfortunately, this view of women is still prevalent in many societies even in the 21st century. From fundamental Islam to presidential elections in the United States, women are judged for how they look and what they wear rather than by what they can do. God's view, however, is not like the world's view. God is interested in

> *The daughters of Zelophehad are right in what they are saying; you shall indeed let them possess an inheritance among their father's brothers and pass the inheritance of their father on to them.*
> *(Numbers 27:7)*

people who will allow grace to move them towards justice, according to God's will, and who have a desire to move others to do the same. God does not place limitations on who can lead, and God had called Deborah to be judge of Israel. Deborah was able to respond to her call because her husband supported her leadership role and the people valued her judgment. Their response to Deborah's leadership was a response to God's grace, which ultimately leads the people to justice.

◯ What are some of the reasons for continued discrimination against women in leadership roles and positions?

JUSTICE UNDER A TREE (Judges 4: 5)

For twenty years the people of Israel had been experiencing oppression by the Canaanites who were under the rule of King Jabin. Jabin's commander, Sisera, had nine hundred iron chariots at his disposal. The Hebrews were barely out of the stage of being a nomadic society, traveling from place to place. Not yet truly a nation, they represented loosely connected bands of tribes. They did not have the structure to fight the well-organized and funded armies of a people who had been in the land for centuries. They were still fighting among one another. This was the purpose of the judge in Hebrew culture, to settle family and tribal arguments.

Let them sit as judges for the people at all times; let them bring every important case to you, but decide every minor case themselves. (Exodus 18: 22a)

Unlike judges that we see on television who wear black robes, control the courtroom with a gavel, and sit on benches behind a tall desk, Deborah sat under a tree. The tree was a date palm tree that grew between two towns in the hill country of the territory of the tribe of Ephraim. In later years of Israel's history, this would be considered the northern kingdom. People would come to her to settle their arguments. Deborah also sat in the middle of very difficult times, but she did not hide behind position or status when looking on the suffering of her people. She understood that the power that she had was not her own; it was God's grace dwelling on the inside of her.

Being a leader means having a willing spirit to follow God and stand up for what is right. Deborah was such a leader, and we, too, have the awesome responsibility to seek justice even in the midst of oppression. Deborah became powerful by being the in midst of those she sought to help. So when God reveals a plan of deliverance for the Hebrew people, a plan that includes the leadership of another person, Deborah is ready. She is ready to do whatever is necessary for the plan to be successful.

1. What character traits should a good and effective leader possess?
2. How can Christians build these traits in themselves and in others?

JUSTICE ON A HIGHWAY

Race, color, ethnicity, gender, and class are not determining factors in God's selection process. During the Civil Rights Movement, God not only called persons like Martin Luther King, Jr. and James Lawson, God called Myles Horton (see Lesson 4), and Gloria Richardson to stand for justice. They allowed the Spirit of God to move them down highways and through cities to protest against injustices. They were unlikely leaders.

Gloria Richardson was an unlikely leader in that she was a parent working as part of a student organization, SNCC (Student Nonviolent Coordinating Committee). At the same time, as a graduate of Howard University and daughter and granddaughter of local business owners, she was also from the "traditionally cautious local black elite, who rarely engaged in any political protest." Yet, she suffered and fought with the people. Richardson was in the midst of her people. She came into the forefront in 1962, organizing the Cambridge Nonviolent Action Committee (CNAC) in the wake of injustice against African diplomats. Highway 50 which went through her town of Cambridge on Maryland Eastern Shore was a rest stop for persons traveling between points north and Washington DC. (Interstate highways were in the process of being built.) When African diplomats traveling from the United Nations in New York City to their embassies in Washington, DC were denied service and assaulted at lunch counters there, it proved to be an embarrassment to a Kennedy White House, promoting so-called freedom and democracy to newly independent African countries.

After an incident in which white police went on a rampage through the black community with gunfire, Richardson stated, "Unless something is achieved soon in Cambridge, then no one is going to be able to control these people who have been provoked by generations of segregation, by countless indignities—and now by uncontrollable white mobs in the streets." During this local and global battle against oppression, Gloria Richardson was part of a compromise brokered by national leaders, including Martin Luther King, Jr. However, the local government would not implement the plan without a vote. Richardson felt that this tactic was unjust and an affront to the dignity of black people. She said, "A first-class citizen does not beg for freedom." Richardson also recognized that there was more to the Movement than a cup of coffee. She expanded the agenda of (CNAC) to include issues of housing, healthcare, and education. Richardson fought and worked with others for God's justice in her community and in the world.

1. Where were you during the Civil Rights Movement?
2. What were some of the events that occurred in your community and how have they influenced your life then, and now?
3. Did you participate or do you know someone who participated in the demonstrations?

EMPOWERED TO EMPOWER (Judges 4: 6-10, 12-16)

As a prophet and judge endowed with power to speak on God's behalf, Deborah was called upon to empower someone else. First, God instructed Deborah to summon Barak from his home, north of her in Kedesh. Apparently, it was the northern region that was having the problem with the Canaanites at this time. Having heard the cries of the people, God communicated a plan of deliverance through Deborah to be carried out by Barak. He was to gather the troops from the northern tribes of Naphtali and Zebulun onto high ground at Mount Tabor and the LORD would direct Sisera's army into low ground, the Wadi or River Kishon (a wadi is a dried creek/river bed) for an Israelite victory. God used Deborah to speak over Barak's life. Deborah spoke to Barak and revealed to him that God had called him to lead the Israelite forces against Sisera's technologically advanced army.

Barak must have been amazed and would not go it alone. Whether out of fear or out of wisdom, he wanted Deborah to accompany him. Deborah indicated that she would indeed go, reminding Barak that the outcome was not for his glory, anyway. The outcome pointed to the leadership of a woman to the glory of God. Barak had the skills to do the task (God would not have chosen him otherwise), but he would not do it without God's representative. Many people have the power and ability to do great things for God, but like Barak need someone to encourage and stand in solidarity with them to feel more comfortable and secure. Many need that extra push to actualize the potential on the inside. We need to be encouraged! When we are encouraged, we feel empowered, and can empower others by God's grace that moves us towards justice.

And let us consider how to provoke one another to love and good deeds, not neglecting to meet together . . . but encouraging one another. (Hebrews 10: 24-25)

Before swooping down the mountain onto Sisera's army below, Deborah again spoke for God, charging Barak to go forward and be totally dependent on God. "God is going before you," she said and Barak was empowered to conquer Sisera's mighty army. When we allow the word of God to ignite the power of the Holy Spirit within us, God will propel us ever forward to the next level. As we grow in grace, let us use the power God has given us to empower others.

1. Name someone who has mentored you or encouraged you and thereby made a lasting impact on your life.
2. What role, specifically, did that person play in your present circumstances or in what you consider a major success story in your life?

BY THE HAND OF A WOMAN (Judges 4: 9, 11, 17-22)

When Deborah told Barak that Israel would be delivered by the hand of a woman, it was not a word of discouragement or judgment; it was a word of prophecy. God had already set things up so that Jael, the wife of Heber the Kenite was in place to capture the escaping Sisera. Deborah believed in the word of God. She knew that God had prepared the way for Barak to be successful. By accompanying him, she strengthens him, allowing him to lead the army of Israel to victory. Sisera was going to be taken care of by someone else, another woman. And indeed we can see that throughout the Bible and throughout history, God has used women to not only strengthen the hands of others but in being spokespersons and leaders in their own right.

There were many women who played a critical role in Freedom Movements. There was Harriet Tubman who escaped slavery in the same county where Gloria Richardson lived and led many on the Underground Railroad to freedom farther north. There was Sojourner Truth, who after her manumission from slavery in New York State, preached God's word of liberation for Blacks and for women. There was Miriam Makeba who sang freedom songs in South Africa until the apartheid government banished her. And there was Ella Baker, whose strong organizational skills were indispensable in building up the NAACP, and in helping to organize the SCLC, SNCC, and the Mississippi Freedom Democratic Party in 1968.

The MFD Party forced rules to be changed on the governance of the Democratic Party that influenced the experience of freedom for all, forty years later. The rules of inclusion were critical to the 2008 election of another Barak, Barack Obama, the first African American President of the United States.

> *Therefore, since we are surrounded by so great a cloud of witnesses, let us also lay aside every weight and the sin that clings so closely, and let us run with perseverance the race that is set before us, looking to Jesus the pioneer and perfecter of our faith, who for the sake of the joy that was set before him endured the cross, disregarding its shame, and has taken his seat at the right hand of the throne of God.*
> (Hebrews 12:1-2)

Gloria Richardson had been taught by her teachers that the power God has given to us is not in the hands of others; it is on the inside of us. As attributed to another woman growing up on Maryland Eastern Shore, she believed: "You have within you the strength, the patience, and the passion to reach for the stars to change the world" (Harriet Tubman). When Jesus called the first disciples, he "gave them power over unclean spirits, to cast them out, and to heal all kinds of sickness and all kinds of disease (Matthew 10:1)." We must believe that we have this power. By faith, whether male or female, and surely by working together as did Deborah and Barak, we have the power to deliver people from injustice and all kinds of evil. By keeping our hands in the hand of Almighty God, we can move from a place of oppression to a place of freedom, justice, and love.

1. Who are women who have impacted your church or community in a positive way?
2. What are ways in which men and women have worked together to bring healing to a community problem?

Closing Prayer: As you meditate on the words of the freedom song, "Come and Go to that Land," thank God for faithful, courageous leaders and pray for the coming of God's kingdom in freedom and justice for all.

Session #2

The Suffering Servant: Moving with God Towards Greatness

Genesis: 39:1-2; 41:14-21,25,39-40

Key Verse *The LORD was with him; and whatever he did, the LORD made it prosper. (Genesis 39:23b)*

Opening Prayer *Loving God, we know that you never send trouble but you work within and through your people in spite of it. By the movement of your Holy Spirit, make your presence known in our lives and in our community in these troubling times. In the name of Jesus Christ. Amen.*

BIBLE LESSON

Now Joseph was taken down to Egypt, and Potiphar, an officer of Pharaoh, the captain of the guard, an Egyptian, bought him from the Ishmaelites who had brought him down there. The LORD was with Joseph, and he became a successful man; he was in the house of his Egyptian master. Then Pharaoh sent for Joseph, and he was hurriedly brought out of the dungeon. When he had shaved himself and changed his clothes, he came in before Pharaoh. And Pharaoh said to Joseph, "I have had a dream, and there is no one who can interpret it. I have heard it said of you that when you hear a dream you can interpret it." Joseph answered Pharaoh, "It is not I; God will give Pharaoh a favorable answer." Then Pharaoh said to Joseph, "In my dream I was standing on the banks of the Nile; and seven cows, fat and sleek, came up out of the Nile and fed in the reed grass. Then seven other cows came up after them, poor, very ugly, and thin. Never had I seen such ugly ones in all the land of Egypt. The thin and ugly cows ate up the first seven fat cows, but when they had eaten them no one would have known that they had done so, for they were still as ugly as before. Then I awoke." Then Joseph said to Pharaoh, "Pharaoh's dreams are one and the same; God has revealed to Pharaoh what he is about to do." So Pharaoh said to Joseph, "Since God has shown you all this, there is no one so discerning and wise as you. You shall be over my house, and all my people shall order themselves as you command; only with regard to the throne will I be greater than you."

DESTINED FOR GREATNESS (Genesis 37: 1-8, 25-28)

As Jacob's favorite son, Joseph knew that he was special. The beautiful coat given him by his father and the dreams that God sent (Genesis 37:5-10), helped him to know that he was, perhaps, destined for greatness. In reality, Joseph had no concept of the meaning of true greatness. Can you imagine the ego on this teenage boy who was handsome and filled with potential, walking around with a coat of many colors, talking about dreams in which representations of his family members were bowing down to him? And his father sent him to supervise over and spy on his older brothers (37:12-14)! No wonder his brothers hated him so!

The greatest among you will be your servant. All who exalt themselves will be humbled, and all who humble themselves will be exalted.
(Matthew 23: 11-12)

Like Joseph, we have been called to be great. God's gracious love reveals God's purpose and plan for our lives in moving us towards greatness. Often, however, we misunderstand what that means. Many think that greatness means being served, but like Joseph, we should discover that greatness means being a servant. God's desire for us to have greatness is connected with our role in God's plan of salvation and deliverance for all people. God gives Joseph-type personalities opportunities to get their understanding of greatness in perspective and make them useable for the kingdom of God.

○ Describe a world-view of greatness using single words. They can be nouns or adjectives.

MOVING WITH GOD TOWARDS GREATNESS

Experiencing greatness of soul in God requires that we grow in the grace of God. Having greatness is not instantaneous; it is a process that often involves painful situations. In order to understand the meaning of true greatness, Joseph needed to go through a process that only hard circumstances could teach him.

1. Infuriated by Jacob's favoritism and Joseph's expressions of grandeur (in sharing his dreams), Joseph's brothers were going to kill him. Instead, they sold him into slavery to the Ishmaelites. The Ishmaelites sold him to the Egyptians. He was seventeen years old. (37: 18-28, 36)

2. As a slave to Potiphar, his abilities were obvious and he was given great responsibility. Potiphar's wife tried to seduce him but he was honorable. Scorned, she lied on him and he ended up in prison on a false rape charge. (39: 1-20)
3. Yet even in prison, Joseph's abilities shine through and he is given great responsibility by the prison guard. In prison his dream-gift resurfaces and Joseph rightly interprets the dreams of two of Pharaoh's servants, one of whom returns to court. (40:1-20)
4. Forgotten, Joseph remains in prison until Pharaoh has two dreams that no one on his staff could interpret. After interpreting the dreams with his God-given gifts, Joseph is elevated from slave and prisoner to prime minister of Egypt. (41:1-57)

Joseph learned important lessons on his journey to greatness. He learned to be humble, to provide excellent service, to have a good attitude, and most of all, to give glory to God from whence all of his gifts and abilities came. Joseph must have had moments that he did not feel so great. He probably felt alone. He may have even believed that God had forgotten all about him at times. Nevertheless, negative things were external to God's favor and grace, which worked for him, in him, and through him in his journey towards greatness.

1. Talk about ways in which God uses the circumstances of our lives to prepare us for greatness.
2. What would you do if you were wrongfully incarcerated as Joseph was?

YOU LOOK GREAT!

Just as it is evident that some people, like Joseph, are set aside to do great things, there are many people whose greatness is unrecognized because of racism and class prejudice. God sees greatness differently from humans. God chose our parents, gender, skin color, personality, and other characteristics. These attributes, however, are incidental in a journey towards greatness. Yet, creating artificial categories of superiority and inferiority happens whenever there is oppression, whether between men/women, Japanese/Chinese, Irish/English, Hutu/Tutsi or Black/White. During slavery, Africans/African Americans were made to feel that they had no potential for greatness, that because they were black, they were incapable of learning and becoming thinkers. Many learned that they could only be great at using their bodies to serve those in power.

These erroneous, unchristian ideologies became racism; fostering a belief that darkness of skin color meant that you did not look great. Nor could you could attain greatness in society. However, even during slavery and Jim Crow, there were black doctors, inventors, writers, architects, artists, and scholars. Nelson Mandela was a lawyer during South African apartheid. Greatness is defined by the power of God that lies on the inside of persons and their willingness to serve God. Many people do not realize their own potential for greatness because they are looking at themselves through the lens of the world and not God. However, all of us are made in the image of God, and we all look great!

I praise you, for I am fearfully and wonderfully made.
(Psalm 139:14a)

1. What does it mean to be created in the image and likeness of God?
2. In what ways can we bring value and dignity to all people?

GREAT IS GOD'S GRACE!

The sense to feel either inferior or superior can only be overcome by God's grace. This is why many African Americans, despite centuries of abuse, could identify God's grace in the midst of racial prejudice and violence. From those in chattel bondage to the Freedom Movement, people were able to sing, "Woke Up this Morning with my Mind on Jesus/Freedom." Even though they were not free, they still were able to keep focused on the goal and move towards greatness of soul and mind. Faith enables us to experience God's grace, knowing that God is present even in the midst of evil.

No, in all these things we are more than conquerors through him who loved us. For I am convinced that neither death, nor life, nor angels, nor rulers, nor things present, nor things to come, nor powers, nor height, nor depth, nor anything else in all creation, will be able to separate us from the love of God in Christ Jesus our Lord.
(Romans 8:37-39)

It was grace that enabled Septima Poinsette Clark, whom Dr. Martin Luther King, Jr. called the Queen Mother of Civil Rights, to teach on St. Johns Island at the age of eighteen, when the Charleston, SC school system was not hiring Blacks in 1916. On St. Johns Island, she used her gift to teach adult literacy and citizenship. Fourteen people attended the first class, and she taught them literacy skills, which helped them to pass the voter registration test. After finally being hired as a Charleston public school teacher, she lost her job by serving with the "illegal" NAACP. By grace, this became an opportunity to train and influence thousands in Citizenship Schools throughout the South, sponsored first by the Highlander Folk School(See Lesson 4) and then the SCLC. God's grace enabled to her say, "Hating people, bearing hate in your heart . . . never accomplishes anything good." In other words, "You can't hate your neighbor if your mind is stayed on freedom!"

It was by God's grace that Hosea Williams survived innumerable imprisonments because of his work in civil rights. Williams would stand on the Tomochichi Rock in downtown Savannah, encouraging people to wade-in at beaches, sit-in at local restaurants, and ride the "ballot bus." He was nicknamed "Little David" because of life-long activism against gigantic issues of racism, poverty, and civil rights. Despite being beaten by Whites for drinking at the "wrong" water fountain after serving in World War II and on Bloody Sunday, he determined, "I am going to do what I believe is right and Godly." He woke up every morning with his mind stayed on Jesus, walkin' and talkin' with his mind stayed on freedom.

In a world in which even many churches are teaching that having God's favor means that you are in a good situation with money, position, and no problems, and that these things should be our goals in life, we must remember that God's grace is greater than our circumstances. Joseph was a slave and a prisoner. Mrs. Clark had trouble finding and keeping a job. Hosea Williams was beaten and jailed. Jesus was rejected and crucified. None of this meant that God did not favor them. These were situations caused by human evil and sin not of the making of these individuals. God's favor, however, operates in every circumstance; God's grace is equal to any task. Great is God's grace and faithfulness!

I know what it is to be in need, and I know what it is to have plenty. I have learned the secret of being content in any and every situation, whether well fed or hungry, whether living in plenty or in want. (Philippians 4:12)

○ How do you know that you have God's favor?

THE PATHWAY TO GREATNESS

The Civil Rights Movement was more than a political movement designed to level the playing field for African Americans. It was a crusade to bring people together and end oppression; it embodied a proclamation that we are all God's children with significant roles to fulfill in bringing forth God's kingdom. We are heirs to the Kingdom! Every child of God has access to a pathway to greatness through Jesus Christ.

The pathway to greatness requires faith in God. When Joseph interpreted the dreams for Pharaoh, he stated, "It is not I; God will give Pharaoh a favorable answer." Joseph trusted in God and in the gifts God had given him. He glorified God for the opportunity to serve. Anytime we have the opportunity to serve, we have an opportunity to move on the pathway of greatness in God. Greatness has to do with being a servant, giving people a lift to the next level in doing the will of God. Jesus washed the disciples' feet, telling them that the slaves are not greater than their master (John13: 12-16). Jesus expects us to be servants of all, as he was. When the disciples began to argue about who was the greatest, Jesus said, "The greatest among you must become like the youngest, and the leader like the one who serves. For who is greater, the one who is at the table or the one who serves? Is it not the one at the table? But I am among you as the one who serves" (Luke 22:26-27). The pathway to greatness is a pathway of servanthood.

The pathway to greatness requires that we allow God's Holy Spirit to work in us. Pharaoh reflected that Joseph had the spirit of God in him. It was a spirit of wisdom, humility, and compassion. The Holy Spirit perfects in us the image of Jesus Christ so that we can have the same mind as Jesus Christ.

"Who, though he was in the form of God,
did not regard equality with God
as something to be exploited,
but emptied himself,
taking the form of a slave
being born in human likeness.
And being found in human form,
he humbled himself
and became obedient to the point of death,
even death on a cross." (Philippians 2:6-8)

The pathway to greatness is a pathway of humility and holiness.

Joseph and Jesus Christ show us the pathway to greatness, which is through suffering and sacrifice. While Joseph was handsome, the prophet Isaiah says of the suffering servant: "He had no form or majesty that we should look at him, nothing in his appearance that we should desire him" (Isaiah 53:2b). The pathway to greatness will require suffering, being wrongfully accused like Joseph, beaten and jailed like Williams, being fired and persecuted like Mrs. Clark. Again, of the suffering servant Isaiah says: "He was despised and rejected by others; a man of suffering (sorrows) and acquainted with infirmity . . . he was despised, and we held him of no account" (Isaiah 53:3). As followers of Jesus, we must share in his suffering in moving towards the abundant life of God's kingdom. Through sacrifice and suffering we grow in greatness of soul, mirroring the image of God within and being made useful in drawing others into wholeness.

> *Little children, you are from God, and have conquered them; for the one who is in you is greater than the one who is in the world.*
> *(1 John 4:4)*

We are made in the image of God! We are created for greatness! And we will surely share in Christ's glory! "We suffer with him so that we might be glorified with him" (Romans 8:17b). Our suffering and our service, like that of Joseph is not in vain. It is redemptive suffering so that God's favor and glory will be revealed in moving others and ourselves towards greatness in Jesus Christ!

What are the benefits of suffering and trials, and how might they affect one's faith and spiritual maturity?

Closing Prayer: As you meditate on the words of the freedom song, "Woke Up This Morning with My Mind Stayed on Freedom," thank God for those who endured suffering for the cause of justice and pray for those who suffer and struggle for the cause of Christ in the 21st century.

Session #3

God's Abundant Kingdom: Moving with Jesus Towards Blessing

Luke 9:10-17; Matthew 14:21

Key Verse *And all ate and were filled. (Luke 9:17a)*

Opening Prayer
Miracle-Working God, move in us to work miracles through us. Teach us how to share with all who have need. In the name of Jesus Christ. Amen.

BIBLE LESSON

On their return the apostles told Jesus all they had done. He took them with him and withdrew privately to a city called Bethsaida. When the crowds found out about it, they followed him; and he welcomed them, and spoke to them about the kingdom of God, and healed those who needed to be cured. The day was drawing to a close, and the twelve came to him and said, "Send the crowd away, so that they may go into the surrounding villages and countryside, to lodge and get provisions; for we are here in a deserted place." But he said to them, "You give them something to eat." They said, "We have no more than five loaves and two fish unless we are to go and buy food for all these people." For there were about five thousand men. And he said to his disciples, "Make them sit down in groups of about fifty each." They did so and made them all sit down. And taking the five loaves and the two fish, he looked up to heaven, and blessed and broke them, and gave them to the disciples to set before the crowd. And all ate and were filled. What was left over was gathered up, twelve baskets of broken pieces.

And those who ate were about five thousand men, besides women and children.

GOD'S ABUNDANT KINGDOM

From the feeding of the Hebrews in the wilderness, to the prophet Elisha's feeding of one hundred (2 Kings 4: 42-44), to Jesus' breakfast by the sea after his resurrection (John 21:4-14), miraculous feedings make manifest the kingdom of God. God promises the hungry shall be fed (Luke 6:21), and those who hunger and thirst after righteousness will be filled (Matthew 5:6). There are many stories in the Gospels about food. Jesus' first miracle involved providing wine for a wedding feast (John 12:1-11). He sat at table to eat meals with friend and foe (Luke 14: 7-14,). Feasting is a metaphor for the kingdom of God (Luke 14:15-24, Matthew 22:1-14). He would not go to the cross until he had sat down to eat a final meal with his friends.

The miracle of the loaves and fishes is the only one of Jesus' miracles that is reported in all four Gospels (Matthew 14:13-21, Mark 6:30-44, John 6:1-14). It is God's desire that people should have enough to eat and that they should be able to eat and be filled. To be physically and emotionally satisfied is a characteristic of God's abundant kingdom.

POSITIONED TO BE A BLESSING! (Luke 9:1-6, 10-12)

A disciple is one who is learning the way of a teacher. Disciples are being equipped to carry out and to continue in that which they have learned. Part of the discipling process is that the student will follow the teachings and orders of the teacher. Additionally, sooner or later, a disciple will have to step out and do things without the teacher being around. Jesus had sent his disciples among the people to proclaim the Gospel of the Kingdom, giving them power and authority to heal, cast out demons and to cure diseases. The disciples were embarking on their first adventures—healing the sick, rebuking demons, and curing diseases.

Upon their return, they were like children coming home from an activity, excited about telling their parents all about it. Jesus took the apostles away to a city called Bethsaida. However, they could not escape the crowd. The crowd found Jesus. Jesus had compassion on the people and preached to them; they looked to him like lost sheep. When Jesus finished teaching, the disciples wanted to get rid of the people because they did not have enough money to feed them. Here, they were in a position to truly show the abundance of God's kingdom by offering them food and even though they had just performed miracles, the disciples did not believe that they could feed the crowd. Rather than acting like apostles—that is—those who had been sent, they behaved as though they had no authority. They were in a position to fulfill the needs of the people but they did not understand it.

GOD PROVIDES THE BLESSING (Luke 9: 13-17)

Jesus orders the disciples to feed the people. He had given them authority and power to proclaim the kingdom of God. Food and sustenance are a manifestation of God's abundant kingdom. Claiming the ability to feed more than 5,000 people was simply another lesson in discipleship. The story as told in Matthew lets us know that there were more than 5, 000. It tells us that in addition to 5,000 men, there were women and children (Matthew 14:21).

When the disciples had gone on their adventure, they were instructed not to take any personal resources but to depend on God and on the generosity of the people. To feed a crowd of people, in their minds, would cost them some money. They were in an economic dilemma. We often find ourselves in the same situation. We may want to help the homeless, make a donation to the youth, give to the poor saints, but when we dig into our pockets, we come up with lint. The disciples had a reality check; ministry requires finances. But Jesus shows them that there are always enough resources to do God's work.

For which of you, intending to build a tower, does not first sit down and estimate the cost, to see whether he has enough to complete it?
(Luke 14:28)

The disciples had not taken stock of what they did have. They were not short of food; they were short of faith. Jesus told them to feed the people; Jesus would provide the means by which that could be done. After a search, they found five loaves of bread and two fishes. The story as told in John (6:1-15) reports that these items came from a child's lunch. The disciples then organized the people as Jesus had instructed. The food was in the hands of Jesus. He looked to heaven, and breaking bread, offered a blessing. Needless to say, there was enough for all, with leftovers. Sitting in groups of fifty ensured that no one in this large crowd would be left out. Jesus taught the disciples to have faith in what God can do through them. They learned that there was a connection between food and ministry.

In what ways can the demonstration of God's love through blessing others influence persons in moving towards salvation?

A STORY OF BLESSING

In doing ministry, it is important to take stock of one's resources. During the Civil Rights Movement, the people of Mississippi discovered that there is a connection between being organized and having enough to eat. As a strategy for effectiveness in a mostly rural and small-town political structure, the various civil rights organizations (NAACP, SNCC, SCLC, CORE) gathered under one banner called COFO (Council of Federated Organizations), working together to share resources and abilities. Thus unified, they decided to concentrate on voter registration in order to empower the people to change a corrupt system based on white supremacy. In spite of arrests and death threats they continued a voting registration crusade, but they met a challenge. There was a food shortage. As the disciples learned that food and ministry is connected, the people of Mississippi learned that there is "connection between political participation and food on their table" (Bob Moses).

In 1963, a cold winter left many sharecroppers without enough food. A federal surplus-food distribution program served as a vital resource in feeding the community, but the county would not distribute the food to Blacks because of the voter registration efforts. This shortage of food and other events inspired over two hundred people to register to vote. This was phenomenal because the earlier efforts of COFO had registered few voters. Additionally, COFO workers responded to the food shortage by organizing a food distribution program, and they gathered "five loaves and two fishes" from northern supporters. Comedian Dick Gregory utilized money from the sale of his records to send a planeload of food and clothes to the distribution center. People would register to vote and collect the things that they needed to live. Through commitment, organization and a willingness to share, people were able to be fed and experience the abundance of God's kingdom.

> Why are organization and cooperation important as we use our God-given gifts to bless the church, community, or nation?

BLESSED TO BE A BLESSING

God uses human agency to move communities towards blessing. Jesus charges us to feed the hungry, to heal the sick, and even to raise the dead. He clothes us so that we can clothe others. He feeds us so that we can feed others. Jesus saves us to so that we can be channels of deliverance for others, moving them towards salvation in Jesus Christ. We are blessed to be a blessing.

Those of us experiencing the grace of God must share this same grace with others. Often we become so consumed with getting for ourselves, receiving blessings, shouting "Increase, increase!" that we forget that we have a responsibility for one another. John Wesley reminds us that being a good steward over our resources is more than making money and saving, but it also means giving. He said, "Earn all you can. Save all you can. Give all you can." We are blessed to be blessing. The purpose of our blessing is not to drive big cars, lounge in our fine homes, and be on the cover of magazines. God has provided us with abundance so that we can share it with others. The song is true; the more you give, the more God gives to you. We cannot beat God's giving. We are blessed to be a blessing.

> *Heal the sick, cleanse the lepers, raise the dead, cast out demons. Freely you have received, freely give.*
> (Matthew 10: 8 NKJV)

If we just take the time to look around, we will be surprised at the abundance we have. If we put our trust in God, we will realize that we have enough money to feed the hungry, to provide healthcare to everyone, to provide adequate housing, and to ensure that everyone has the opportunity to attend college without being concerned about financial debt. Jesus tells disciples to feed the people. He proves that there are enough resources. If there are resources enough to fund wars, to buy guns, for a nation to be overweight, to drive gas-guzzling cars, then there are resources to keep colleges and hospitals open, to keep people in their homes and in school, and to create jobs for all who want to work. We are blessed to be a blessing!

1. Discuss this definition of blessing: "Something promoting or contributing to happiness, well-being and /or prosperity." (*American Heritage Dictionary*)
2. How have you used the blessings in your life to bless someone else?

GOD WANTS TO BLESS EVERYBODY

We must cooperate, be organized, and be led by God in order to build up a community in which the blessings of God are accessible to all. The twelve apostles were probably overwhelmed by the logistical problem of having to feed so many people. But through God's blessing and a system of provision, all were fed. When faced with a problem of food scarcity, COFO could have been overwhelmed, but through others being willing to use their blessings to bless someone else and through an organizational process, they had a system for servicing those in need, thereby doing God's will. When the physical needs of the people were met, they were able to see the importance of political action. In the same way, when we provide for the physical and spiritual needs of people in the community, they will see the importance of having a relationship with Jesus Christ.

> *Bring the full tithe into the storehouse, so that there may be food in my house, and thus put me to the test, says the Lord of hosts; see if I will not open the windows of heaven for you and pour down for you an overflowing blessing.* (Malachi 3:10)

We are all dependent on God's daily grace and provision. A relationship with God helps us to be thankful for what we have and to understand God's love and care for us. God wants to bless us so that we can heal the sick, feed the hungry, clothe the naked, and to move with Jesus towards blessing, personal deliverance and deliverance to the community. If we are willing to share God's blessings with others, God will give us the increase and take us to new levels in our faith and our relationship with God.

During the Civil Rights Movement, there were very few monetary resources to get out information, to lead demonstrations, yet everybody was singing and calling out for freedom! In the midst of scarcity, those who had been materially blessed by God, shared with others, so that they could pass on the blessing by becoming whole citizens in society and in God's kingdom. We do not need to play the lottery or send in prayer cloths and a donation to walk in the blessings of God. Blessing is God's will. We just have to believe in what God can do with our "two fishes and five loaves of bread," be good stewards, and be willing to share the abundance of God's kingdom.

1. In what ways should accountability be the standard in the life of a Christian?
2. Why do you think God requires accountability from God's people?

Closing Prayer: As you meditate on the words of the freedom song, "Everybody Sing 'Freedom!'" be thankful for God's providence and pray that God's abundance will be experienced by all.

Session #4

True Treasure: Moving with God Towards Truth

1 Kings 10:1-10,13 (NIV)

Key Verse *Strive first for the kingdom of God and its righteousness, and all these things will be given to you as well. (Matthew 6:33 NRSV)*

Opening Prayer *All-Wise God, give us an appetite for truth that surpasses that which we have for food, for power or for things. By your Holy Spirit, move us to value the things that you consider important and to give less attention to things that will fade away. In the name of Jesus Christ. Amen.*

BIBLE LESSON

When the queen of Sheba heard about the fame of Solomon and his relation to the name of the LORD, *she came to test him with hard questions. Arriving at Jerusalem with a very great caravan—with camels carrying spices, large quantities of gold, and precious stones—she came to Solomon and talked with him about all that she had on her mind. Solomon answered all her questions; nothing was too hard for the king to explain to her. When the queen of Sheba saw all the wisdom of Solomon and the palace he had built, the food on his table, the seating of his officials, the attending servants in their robes, his cupbearers, and the burnt offerings he made at the temple of the* LORD *she was overwhelmed. She said to the king, "The report I heard in my own country about your achievements and your wisdom is true. But I did not believe these things until I came and saw with my own eyes. Indeed, not even half was told me; in wisdom and wealth you have far exceeded the report I heard. How happy your men must be! How happy your officials, who continually stand before you and hear your wisdom! Praise be to the* LORD *your God, who has delighted in you and placed you on the throne of Israel. Because of the* LORD's *eternal love for Israel, he has made you king, to maintain justice and righteousness." And she gave the king 120 talents of gold, large quantities of spices, and precious stones. Never again were so many spices brought in as those the queen of Sheba gave to King Solomon. King Solomon gave the queen of Sheba all she desired and asked for, besides what he had given her out of his royal bounty. Then she left and returned with her retinue to her own country.*

THE WISDOM OF SOLOMON (1 Kings 3:1-28)

King Solomon was the wisest and richest king during Israelite history. When he began his reign as king of Israel, Solomon prayed to God for wisdom (1 Kings 3: 5-9). He wanted to be able to discern the truth concerning the people under his leadership. Solomon had his priorities in order. Solomon's wisdom was proven by his first case (1 Kings 3: 16-28). It involved two prostitutes who both had baby boys within three days of one another. One mother rolled over on her baby in the middle of the night, killing him. In the attempt to cover up the death of her child, she switched the dead baby with the live child of the other woman. Solomon made a show of deciding the maternity of the living child by ordering the baby split in two. The real mother protested this ruling by relinquishing her claim to the baby. Solomon awarded her the child, understanding that the true mother would rather have someone else raising her child than have him killed. This landmark case earned Solomon a reputation among his people for being wise and able to discern the truth. It was a reputation that spread throughout the earth.

People came from all the nations to hear the wisdom of Solomon; they came from all the kings of the earth who had heard of his wisdom. (1 Kings 4:34)

1. How can we learn to discern the truth?
2. Where do you go to get wisdom?

THE JOURNEY OF A QUEEN (1 Kings 10:1-2)

The queen of Sheba was a powerful woman. Her kingdom spanned present-day Yemen across the strait into Africa, inclusive of present-day countries such as Ethiopia, Somalia, Eritrea, Djibouti, what is known as the Horn of Africa. The religious and historical records of Ethiopia have information about their queen's visit to Israel. Jesus called her the queen of the South and praised her for coming from the ends to the earth to seek wisdom.

Like other royal figures throughout the earth at that time, the queen of Sheba had heard about King Solomon. His relationship with God is what had caused him to rise so quickly. As the head of state controlling trade routes going to and from the Middle East, Asia and Africa, the queen needed to know more about Solomon and Israel. People had talked about Solomon—his money and his wisdom. She wanted to know if what she heard was true. She did not want to rely on the rumors, but she wanted to discover the truth for herself. She knew that the truth would not come to her; she had to venture out to attain it. In the ancient world, kings and queens would test each other's wits by posing questions which answers required some discernment—riddles. It was basically a contest, a game of jeopardy. On this journey, she brought gifts for King Solomon and many questions.

By what means do the world leaders of today seek truth and wisdom?

A QUEST FOR TRUTH (1 Kings 10: 3-9)

The queen's quest for the truth was not purely motivated by curiosity. It was her responsibility to gain an understanding as to the source of Solomon's wealth, wisdom, and power. The queen of Sheba asked hard questions to which King Solomon gave satisfactory answers. She was given a tour of his palaces and the newly-built temple. She gained access to everything concerning his material wealth and power, and his faithfulness to God. As she made her tour, she could see that Solomon treated his people with the justice and righteousness of God, no matter their station. She saw how from the highest (his wives) to the lowliest (his servants and valets) everyone was happy, well-dressed, well-fed, and with opportunity for an education at the feet of Solomon. Now she had first-hand experience, having seen everything with her own eyes, and what she had seen left her breathless. She had no more questions.

Buy truth, and do not sell it; buy wisdom, instruction, and understanding. (Proverbs 23:23)

The queen of Sheba attributed Solomon's success to God's favor and blessing. After being blown away with Solomon's situation, she acknowledged the anointing God placed on Solomon. She praised the God of Israel for having set him on the throne. Solomon's position in life was an indication of God's love for the people and nation of Israel. God placed a person of wisdom, discernment, and intelligence as the leader of the country and this black woman was most impressed. She believed that Solomon was a man who would continue to be just in his dealings and faithful in his engagements, trying always to do what was right in the eyes of the Lord.

This is what Jesus meant when he said, "Strive first for the kingdom of God and its righteousness, and all these things will be given to you as well."(Matthew 6:33) Solomon's desire for wisdom and righteousness gave him access to treasure of all kinds, human resources and material resources.

God's Grace from Place to Place Student

This is what impressed the queen; God was a priority in Solomon's life and so God made Solomon a priority. God's grace had moved her towards a greater truth, the revelation that the God of Israel was real. She realized that she was in the presence of royalty greater than Solomon --- God! God's grace always leads to this truth, the existence of God and the realness of Jesus Christ. The queen of Sheba understood that wisdom and faith are the greatest treasure.

Happy are those who find wisdom, and those who get understanding, for her income is better than silver, and her revenue better than gold. (Proverbs 3:13)

1. What do you value most in life and how do you know that it is your greatest treasure?
2. What are some spiritual disciplines that help us to make God a priority in our lives?

THE TREASURE OF GOD'S TRUTH (1 Kings 10:10)

The queen of Sheba observed that those in Solomon's court were happy not only because their material needs were being met, they were happy because their spiritual and educational needs were being met as well. Myles Horton was a man of faith. Born in Appalachia, he was very aware of how material lack, deep poverty produced a lack of well-being in people. He went on a quest to educate himself on how to empower people through education to move towards justice and economic equity. This quest led him to theological school in New York and to Denmark to study the folk schools there.

First developed in Denmark, folk school is a form of adult education that is based on a cooperative methodology between learners and teachers, emphasizing awareness and appreciation for the needs and values of the community.

In 1932, he established the Highlander Folk School in Monteagle, TN. The center gave knowledge, wisdom, and hands-on experience to gain justice and equity, first for poor white laborers and then to civil rights workers, both black and white, allowing persons to learn about and practice skills on direct action and passive resistance. This man from Appalachia came to believe the great truth of Christianity that he must do unto others as he wants them to do unto him. He put it this way, "Anything I want for myself, I must want for other people." He came to understand that justice for white people was linked with justice for Blacks and that justice for black people would be the salvation of white people. Starting in 1942, until it was shut down (1961) by authorities claiming that it was a communist training school, the Highlander Folk School was a refuge of interracial learning and fellowship. The Highlander reopened in Knoxville, TN in 1961 and then again in 1972 as the Highlander Research and Education Center in New Market, TN, where it remains to this day.

Many people, including Rosa Parks, Dr. King, and students from Historically Black Colleges and Universities and other institutions went to the Highlander. In addition to seeking an education that would prepare them for jobs and careers, students also made a "great discovery of knowledge learned in the streets and beyond the classroom towards a higher understanding of life."* They responded to the truth they were taught. Discussions surrounding the nonviolence movement included whether to stay in jail without bail, sit-ins, and protests. Parks, through the training she learned there in the summer of 1955, refused to move to the back of the bus in the winter. Septima Poinsette Clark taught at Highlander, launching the literacy/citizenship programs that spread all over the South. The anthem of the Civil Rights Movement "We Shall Overcome" was developed there.

By seeking God's truth at the Highlander School, many were equipped in the fight to overcome ignorance, poverty, and oppression. They were in a position to give and share the truth with others. Unlike the lavish treasure the queen of Sheba gave to Solomon, their gifts were priceless; they gave their time (sometimes spent in jail), tireless efforts, their bodies to be beaten, and even their lives in order to move society closer to an ideal of God's truth.

1. In what ways did the Civil Rights Movement open doors of education and opportunity for African Americans, women, and other minorities? How have these opportunities affected life for everyone?
2. What educational inequities still exist in American society today?

* from a speech by Rev. C.T. Vivian given at Tennessee State University in September 2008

AND NOTHING BUT THE TRUTH (1 KINGS 10:13)

Many in the religious leadership of Jesus' time were in the presence of the truth but they did not know it. Rather than exploring the truth, they did not want to believe the truth of Jesus the Christ. Rather than questioning in a manner that would open their minds to the truth, as the queen of Sheba did, they were always trying to trap him. When they demanded that he prove his kingship, Jesus tells them that the queen of Sheba will rise up in judgment against them.

> *"The queen of the south shall rise up in the judgment with this generation, and shall condemn it: for she came from the uttermost parts of the earth to hear the wisdom of Solomon; and, behold, a greater one than Solomon is here".*
> (Matthew 12:42)

When the queen of Sheba left the presence of King Solomon, she did not leave the truth behind. She had met a great king and learned the truth of his wealth and wisdom. She carried the treasure of truths learned in his court with her. Yet, we have someone greater than Solomon among us; we have Jesus Christ, who is the truth. He is with us all the time. If we believe the truth, the truth shall set us free! (John 8: 32) Let us believe in the truth and allow it to penetrate our hearts. The truth is with us all the time, and by allowing the grace of God to draw us closer to the truth, we can share it with others. Jesus is the truth, the whole truth, and nothing but the truth.

1. How and why are we dependent upon the Holy Spirit in the process of revelation of truth?
2. What is the truth of the matter regarding race relations in America today? Did the election of an African American president signal change that has come or a continuing work in progress?

> *I am the way, the truth and the life. No one comes to the Father except through me.* (John 14:6)

Closing Prayer: As you meditate on the words of the freedom song, "We Shall Overcome," thank God for the victories and pray for those who must overcome ignorance, addiction, and economic lack.

Session #5

Grace, Love and Justice:
Moving with Jesus Towards Reconciliation

Acts 15:36-41 and 2 Timothy 4:9-11

Key Verse *First be reconciled to your brother or sister, and then come and offer your gift. (Matthew 5:24b)*

Opening Prayer
Lord, move us to forgive as you forgive, completely and unconditionally. In the name of Jesus Christ. Amen.

BIBLE LESSON

After some days Paul said to Barnabas, "Come, let us return and visit the believers in every city where we proclaimed the word of the Lord and see how they are doing." Barnabas wanted to take with them John called Mark. But Paul decided not to take with them one who had deserted them in Pamphylia and had not accompanied them in the work. The disagreement became so sharp that they parted company; Barnabas took Mark with him and sailed away to Cyprus. But Paul chose Silas and set out, the believers commending him to the grace of the Lord. He went through Syria and Cilicia, strengthening the churches.

Do your best to come to me soon, for Demas, in love with this present world, has deserted me and gone to Thessalonica; Crescens has gone to Galatia, Titus to Dalmatia. Only Luke is with me. Get Mark and bring him with you, for he is useful in my ministry.

God's Grace from Place to Place Student

GRACE FROM PLACE TO PLACE (Acts 15: 36)

Many of us know Paul. He was the man that once persecuted Christians. Then he met Jesus on the way to Damascus, was blinded for three days, and became a champion of the Gospel. Barnabas was also a champion of the Gospel. God had put them together. These two ministers were a strong team. Paul and Barnabas "had been commended to the grace of God for the work" (14:26b), of spreading the Gospel of Jesus Christ by traveling from place to place. They had even traveled to Jerusalem together in order to refute the teaching that Gentiles had to be circumcised in order to become part of the Christian community (Acts 15). Indeed, they formed such a powerful bond that they were ready to go back to the places they had formed churches in order to check on them. How amazing that an argument arose between these close companions!

Traveling from place to place is a mode of promoting grace and reconciliation between God and human beings. The travels of Paul and Barnabas are a precursor of the CORE (Congress of Racial Equality) Journey of Reconciliation that took place under the leadership of James Farmer. Farmer was a member of the debate team at Wiley College (*The Great Debaters*), who after witnessing a brutal lynching became determined to find nonviolent means by which to achieve racial equality and justice. In 1944, Irene Morgan, who was returning to Baltimore after visiting her mother in the Tidewater region of Virginia, refused a request to give up her seat to a white person, also preventing her seat partner (who was carrying a baby) from doing the same. She was arrested and the NAACP took her case to the Supreme Court resulting in Irene Morgan *v.* Commonwealth of Virginia. The 1946 decision by the Court held "that seating arrangements for the different races in interstate motor travel requires a single uniform rule to promote and protect national travel." The 1947 Journey of Reconciliation was to test the 1946 law. It was met with violence.

"If the world hates you, be aware that it hated me before it hated you. If you belonged to the world, the world would love you as its own."
(John 15:18-19a)

In 1961, CORE and SNCC sponsored freedom rides, once again testing the 1946 law. The response, again, was violence. On May 4, 1961, black and white freedom riders divided into two groups, one group on a Greyhound and the other on a Trailways bus. Black people would use white facilities, and white people would use black facilities. Blacks would sit at the front of the bus, and Whites at the back of the bus, testing state laws against federal laws prohibiting segregation. They were spreading the good news of justice and equity, letting people know about the desegregation of interstate transportation. Though God's grace strengthens as we go from place to place, it will face opposition to the message.

> How has God moved you out of your comfort zone to serve by spreading the gospel? What does it mean to be counter-cultural?

ALL RELATIONSHIPS HAVE DISAGREEMENTS
(Acts 15: 37- 38)

After completing their first missionary journey, Paul suggested to Barnabas that they do follow up visits to the cities where they had proclaimed the Word of God. Barnabas was not opposed to this idea of what they should do. The two disagreed with one another about whom they should take. Barnabas wanted to take John Mark, but Paul disagreed with this proposal because John Mark had deserted them on their first trip. Paul did not think that John Mark was dependable, while Barnabas wanted to give him another chance. They were in agreement on the big issue, but they were in disagreement on some small, petty stuff.

It is the nature of evil to be destructive of relationships like the one that existed between Paul and Barnabas. Even the forces of evil understand the importance and power of being unified and work extra hard to disrupt unity. The truth is that in any relationship, there will be disagreements. We need God's grace to enable each person to work through conflict towards reconciliation. We need God's grace to help us to come together.

For I do not do the good I want, but the evil I do not want is what I do. (Romans 7:19)

Just as in the crucifixion and resurrection of Jesus Christ, there is often violence, disruption and a seeming victory of evil before true reconciliation can occur. The 1947 Journey of Reconciliation and the Freedom Rides of 1961 would result in violence and arrests, but they were moving people towards recognizing that it was time to come together. White southerners were afraid of coming together and the fear resulted in violence. The freedom riders did not intend to continue, escalate or encourage the violence; their stance on nonviolence revealed their intentions towards reconciliation. Before getting on these rides, the participants were trained in nonviolence tactics, including how to curl up in order to avoid serious injuries to the body.

1. Why would a movement, like the Civil Rights Movement, to change social mores, customs, and standards require participation of all parts of society?
2. How would a lack of participation prevent unity from coming to the body of Christ?

SMALL STUFF CAN TURN INTO BIG STUFF
(Acts 15: 39-41)

Unfortunately, small, petty stuff can end relationships and destroy teams. It wasn't enough for Paul that Barnabas agreed with his idea, but he wanted to design the whole plan. They became more consumed over their individual likes and dislikes rather than dealing with the big picture of what they were supposed to be doing. When the argument became so deep that they split, the issue was no longer about John Mark, it was about self and winning. They lost focus on what they were supposed to do. Rather than looking at ways to resolve the conflict, the issue grew out of control. Neither one could hear from God because of the anger; they separated and went in opposite directions. Barnabas took John Mark and traveled southwest to the island of Cyprus. Paul chose Silas and departed, traveling over land, south and east through Syria and then north to Cilicia.

Come now, let us reason together, says the LORD.
(Isaiah 1:18, NIV).

Do two walk together unless they have agreed to do so?
(Amos 3:3, NIV)

Churches split over many matters, most of which have nothing to do with doctrine! Friendships split up because of an unwillingness to forgive. Marriages end because at least one person does not want to think about the other person's needs, and parents and children lose contact because of misunderstandings. When Paul and Barnabas separated, the believers commended Paul to the grace of the Lord and he went throughout the region making the churches stronger. The people's prayers for Paul revealed that the persons doing the work were secondary to the work of bringing people to salvation that needed to be done. God's work will go forth in spite of our unwillingness to cooperate and compromise with one another. The work is not about us, but about giving God the glory.

> What does it mean to "have a fellowship of kindred minds . . . like to that above" (*from Blest Be the Ties That Binds*)? What specific practices can move churches toward greater unity?

CONFLICT RESOLUTION, COMPROMISE, AND CHRIST

Although Paul and Barnabas both had good points, the argument was petty and reconciliation was possible. The joint efforts of both Blacks and Whites on the Freedom Rides exemplified that reconciliation between the races was possible. Black and white people can get along; they can live together, they can cooperate with one another. The Freedom Rides and the other civil rights protests were ways to help other people to see this truth. They were designed on the theological premise that regardless of what we look like on the outside, we are all created in the image of God. Through Jesus Christ, we are brothers and sisters.

Conflict resolution requires us to be willing to give up something for the sake of the relationship to reach a compromise. There were possible compromises Paul and Barnabas could have reached. Paul could have agreed to take John Mark on a trial basis. Barnabas could have agreed not to take John Mark to the first couple of cities, and let him join later, or they could have worked out a plan where Paul would take Silas, and Barnabas would take John Mark, and they would split up the cities and connect after the completion of the mission. Compromise is only possible when two people are willing to participate, sacrifice, hold themselves accountable, and focus on Christ rather than their own selfish goals and objectives.

Two people cannot compromise or reconcile if one or both are on the Frank Sinatra "I-did-it-my-way" plan. A "my-way-or-the-highway" method of conflict resolution never works. For true, lasting reconciliation to take place it must

Love is patient; love is kind; love is not envious or boastful or arrogant or rude. It does not insist on its own way.
(1 Corinthians 13: 4-5a)

be God's way with God's grace, love, and justice. From 1843-1844, churches (Baptist, Methodist, Presbyterian, and others) split over the issue of slavery. The southern states wanted their "way of life" and the northern states wanted to abolish slavery. Nevertheless, many of the reasons for pursuing abolition had nothing to do with God's grace, love, and justice.

Many of the same people promoting abolition were also promoting the return of black people to Africa and supported creating Liberia, as a colony, for that purpose. Some supported abolition out of economic concerns. One reason the Civil War went on so long is because the economy of the southern states was based on the free labor of black people. The profits and lifestyle of the southern states represented a low percentage investment. In addition to being a document of justice for an enslaved people, the Emancipation Proclamation was a tactic of war, taking the economic and labor advantage away from the Confederacy. Yet, true justice, grace and love would have guaranteed freed persons their forty acres and a mule instead of Jim Crow.

Therefore, W.E.B. DuBois' prophecy that for America "The problem of the color line is the problem of the 20th century"* remains true even into the 21st century, despite abolition, the Civil Rights Movement, and the election of Barack Obama as president of the United States. Many people did not want to cast a vote for Barack Obama because of his ethnicity and color. They were not opposed to his political views; they were opposed to his race.

* "Of the Dawn of Freedom" *Souls of Black Folks* by W.E. B. DuBois 1903

God's grace, however, does not see color. God's justice is based on what is best for "the least of these." God's love is seamless, all-encompassing, and perfectly inclusive. We are all God's children but reconciliation can only occur when we look at each other with the eyes of God. Otherwise, God's grace cannot move us from a place of division to a place of building up the kingdom of God. Most churches continue to be race-based with even multicultural churches refusing to address the need for the racial healing that should happen in society. We must let go and let God. A good compromise is the result of two parties sacrificing their wants for the betterment of the relationship. To work through conflict and reach a compromise, we need Jesus Christ.

◯ Divide into three groups. Each group will take 2-3 minutes to define either grace, love, or justice.

RECONCILIATION THROUGH JESUS CHRIST
(2 Timothy 4:9-11)

Nevertheless, true healing is more than compromise. It involves repentance from sin. It involves forgiveness for the wrongs and injustices committed. True healing requires a giving up of self as Jesus gave up himself. Just as reconciliation with God means being on one accord with the will of God through the acceptance of Jesus Christ as Savior in spoken and lived witness, reconciliation among human beings means truly wanting for others what you want for yourself and working towards that reality. Jesus Christ can heal relationships. When Jesus Christ brings restoration to relationships, he makes them stronger. Marriages can recover from adultery, churches can avoid division, and friendships can be repaired.

And he died for all, so that those who might live might live no longer for themselves, but for him who died and was raised for them.
(2 Corinthians 5:15)

Barnabas and Paul's relationship not only demonstrates our constant need for God's grace so that we can love and live like Jesus Christ, it shows that the healing process is not instantaneous. The saying that time heals all wounds has truth. It takes a lot of work to hold a grudge and to remember past wrongs. In the case of Paul and Mark, Paul, in his second letter to Timothy, as he is perhaps languishing in a Roman prison, encouraging Timothy to visit him, he goes down a list of missionary companions and tells Timothy to bring Mark. He has a deep appreciation for Mark's gifts, which have been beneficial to the ministry. Paul lets go of his grudge against Mark. Indeed, Paul's ministry of proclamation concerning reconciliation between God and humanity through Jesus Christ is illustrated in the healing of his relationship with Mark. It also reveals that when Jesus repairs relationships, they are not the same. They are more durable because the people involved in them are stronger, wiser, and better as a result of the conflict. When we are willing to look at the people around us as children of God, God's grace can move us toward reconciliation and into a stronger relationship with Jesus Christ.

> *From now on, therefore, we regard no one from a human point of view . . . All this from God, who reconciled us to himself through Christ, and has given us a ministry of reconciliation; that is, in Christ God was reconciling the world to himself, not counting their trespasses against them, and entrusting the message of reconciliation to us.*
> *(2 Corinthians 5:16a, 18-19)*

1. Forgiveness is part of the process of reconciliation. What is forgiveness?
2. How can you promote repentance, forgiveness, and reconciliation in your family? church? community?

Closing Prayer: As you listen to "If You Miss Me from the Back of the Bus," thank God through Jesus Christ, for how African Americans generally have moved from the back of the bus to a better place. Pray for justice for all of God's children.